Stew

Cookbook

Quick and Easy Pressure Cooker Favorite Soup

(A Collection of Delicious Soup Recipes and Stew Recipes to Warm Your Heart)

Edith Maxwell

Published By **Bella Frost**

Edith Maxwell

Stew Cookbook: Quick and Easy Pressure Cooker Favorite Soup (A Collection of Delicious Soup Recipes and Stew Recipes to Warm Your Heart)

ISBN   978-1-998901-48-7

No part of this guidebook shall be reproduced in any form without permission in writing from the publisher except in the case of brief quotations embodied in critical articles or reviews.

Legal & Disclaimer

Table Of Contents

What kind of meat is suitable to braise?

While braising, it's an beneficial that small portions of meat can be delicious and soft. Connective tissue and tendon transform into gelatine.

If the meat isn't lean enough cut it into pieces. To do this, bacon that is fat will be pulled into the meat. You can also let the butcher pull this out for you.

Different types of meats Lamb, poultry, pork, and beef are braised.

Portion of meat: Meat taken from the belly, cheeks legs neck, legs, neck shoulder, ribs, lower shell and tail gets soft and tender.

The amount of meat consumed: approx. 200 g of beef are consumed each day. Take note that if the food has bones in it the weight is to be added together.

The right pots to stew in

The stews can be prepared by baking or stove at a low temperature. It is crucial that the pot has a tight lid, and is as heavy as is possible.

Cast iron grills are well used for braising. They can hold heat well, and ensure that cook the food in a uniform way.

If you don't have as much time, you could cook goulash, pot roast and other dishes in pressure cookers. This reduces the time to cook to about half.

What to look out for when cooking

Searing the meat: First sprinkle the meat in large chunks with salt and black pepper and then sear them with a vigorous heat. smaller pieces of meat for goulash and ragout are seasoning after they've been sear-fried. The meat is fried in pieces. Make sure to not fill the pan completely. The most efficient fat is clarified butter.

Add vegetables: Once the meat is cooked, remove it from the roaster and add the vegetables, carrots onions, and celery. Roast all of it thoroughly. Additionally, a small amount of tomato paste could be baked. Add the meat, and cook using wine or stock.

Liquid: The main aspect of braising is to keep the roast in a constant state of moisture. The roast shouldn't simmer within the sauce. The meat must be cooked to the highest point within the steam or in the middle in the broth. Include a little bit of wine or broth at the beginning and then add it three or two times.

Close the lid. After you've seared the meat and the flame is extinguished, shut the lid. Then , continue to braise by baking in the oven over the stove with a low flame.

The correct cooking time: The meat should not simmer for too long during braising or it could lose its flavor and turn fibrous. If you'd like to verify whether the meat is cooked then place it onto a wooden fork. If it slides down quickly, it's done. A meat thermometer can also do an excellent job. It lets you check the temperatures of your meat. Based on the kind of meat, the temperature is usually between 70-85 degrees. The time to cook depends on the kind of meat, the size, and the quality. For instance beef roulades and goulash must simmer for between two and three hours.

Sauce: In order to make a sauce, pull the meat that has been cooked out of the roaster and place it in a warm oven. The sauce will be blended with the stock as well as the cooked vegetables. The stock may be also poured through an ice-cold sieve before being boiled down. The sauce can be spiced with crème fraiche, whipped cream, sour cream , and spices.

The side dishes of stews The traditional way to serve vegetables is in stews, such as cabbage, like creamy sausages, Brussels sprouts, red cabbage , or green beans. If you're looking for something unique for a dish to serve as a side, you can serve polenta sliced instead of potatoes or mashed potatoes. It is a delicious dish made of corn grits that is delicious with lamb or game.

Freezing Stews can be frozen with no issues. Allow the meat to cool completely following the braising process and then freeze it along with the sauce. It is possible to store it in the freezer for up to 6 months.

What happens when you braise?

Then, grill the meat in each of its sides so that it develops toasted smells and acquire an attractive hue. The cooked vegetables are simmered in a pot, best in the cast iron roaster. The stew is then simmered tightly with a little amount of liquid like alcohol, broth for meat or wine for many hours. The temperature of the pot is in the range of 80-90 temperatures, this being very lower than other cooking methods like grilling or roasting. The meat is cooked smoky by using the steam generated inside the pot that is sealed or below in the brew it itself. This creates a faster temperature than cooking. The collagen transforms into gelatin in it's cooking. The muscle fibers soften and the gelatin ensures the water remains inside the flesh, which makes it soft and succulent.

However, be aware that the kinds of meats can be braised. The lean meat, which contains little to no collagen, can become tough and dry after cooking for long periods. Braising is the best cooking method for meats that are high in collagen like neck of beef, brisket, or ribs.

An oven can be a superior heater as opposed to the stove. Heat is transmitted in indirecteaspoony meaning that the meat cooks slow and evenly. Additionally the braised stock will be more smooth in this manner.

Benefits of braising

1. The meat cooks evenly and is very gentle.

2. The braising is always done with a lid so that the steam remains within the pan. It acts as a heating source.

3. The lengthy cooking time makes an extremely creamy and fragrant sauce.

They're delicious and tasty. When you next have a gathering with your family members on the weekend or on a holiday and have than enough time for cooking, try braising a go.

Amazing facts on stews

Take the roasting ingredients off in the middle of the pan

When the meat pieces are nicely browned remove them from the pan and repeat the roasting process using the vegetables. The combination of celery, onions, and carrots provide a delicious taste. After cooking the vegetables, scrub them clean using an liquid. Broth or stock can be used for this. It is essential that the roasted ingredients separate from the bottom to enhance the flavor of the liquid.

Water or stock

The liquid you choose to deglaze can affect the flavor. It is recommended to look into a veal stock to make stews made from beef and veal. The wine addition is also very popular. Wine that is red works well with beef dishes. It's recommended to make use of white wine when cooking Veal to ensure that the meat doesn't color. The wine must be cooked down thoroughly while the pot is open as otherwise the alcohol flavour may become too strong.

Sauce is a great way to enhance the taste of the meat

The stock is transformed to create a delicious sauce adding additional spices and ingredients that enhance and enhance the flavor that the beef has. It is possible to thicken the sauce by adding the addition of starch, or in a traditional method, by using flour. This option is ideal for when no additional ingredients are needed and the sauce is great. You can also thin the braised sauce by adding crème fraiche or frozen butter. Another proven method to thicken the sauce is boiling it down. The sauce will thicken gradually when the water is removed from it. The vegetables that are passed around are good binding agents and can add a bit of flavor.

Basic methods of preparation include stewing, steaming, and braising

This section will discuss the most frequently used terms for preparation along with their significance: Steaming braising, stewing, and. The various methods typically differ in minor aspects however they all are crucial to the final product.

Basic Preparation Type no.1 Steaming

Steaming is a method of cooking that is particularly gentle. It is perfect for low-fat fish, delicate vegetables , or soft meat. Food prepared using hot steam. The benefits of this method is that the vitamins and minerals remain in the food, and the vegetables remain nice and crisp without being reduced in water. To steam, you need the right pot that has a sieve insertthat keeps the boiling water separate from the food items, or a steamer that is specially designed for the task is needed.

For cooking food, you need to add little bit of water to the pot , and then, place the sieve with the ingredients on it. After that, you can heat the water to the point of boiling (about 100 degrees C). It is essential that the water at this point does not pass through the filter.

2. Basic preparation type. Steaming

Steaming is when food is cooked using only one tablespoon of liquid or it's own juice. Items with large amounts of water are appropriate for this preparation method. A sufficient amount of liquid, stock, or wine is used to cover all the contents of the pan or pot. This type of recipe is also great for eating on a diet since it is very low in fat.

The benefit of this method is that food items that are sensitive such as soft fish and vegetables maintain their intense flavor as well as their color and flavor. They acquire their full-bodied aroma since it is because they cook in the same juices, and thus do not lose their flavor.

Basic Preparation Type no.3 Raising

While cooking, the food is cooked first, and then seared on both sides. This results in roasted smells, which give the food the rich flavor that is characteristic of the cooking process. This technique is commonly used in cooking. Once the meat is cooked, it is then extinguished by using broth, stock or wine. The liquid should be used to cover the roast to ensure that the meat is still juicy as it cooks.

To enhance the flavor To enhance the taste, mushrooms, vegetables, or bacon are also included in the braising process. The food can simmer in the pot that is sealed for several hours, ensuring that the roast becomes as tender like butter. In the end, the liquid can be used as a delicious sauce base.

Side dishes for stews

There are a variety of delicious sides dishes to stews. There are many varieties of vegetables, and dumplings of various kinds are ideal. There are many of them below. A few of the recipes are found in the section on recipes:

1. Vanilla and Carrots are a extremely delicious and tasty accompaniment to stews.

2. Thuringian napkin dumplings - prepare the dumplings with herbs or no. Whatever

you choose, they work extremely well with stews.

3. Puree of parsley root It is a delicious accompaniment to stews or festive roasts. It works especially very well when served with game.

4. Baked herb potatoes The potatoes are very delicious when cooked with stews.

5. Confit onions are a food item that is great with stews, and is very easy to cook.

6. Honey onions : This food item is in the Orient and is in itself stew. It can be served with meat and is great as a meal starter.

7. Mashed carrots and potatoes - A tasty side dish that works well with nearly any stew.

8. Orange gremolata - This dish is great with stews, but it also works with pasta and risotto.

9. Black currants that have been cooled and stirred - perfect for stews, such as venison ragout, breaded pork schnitzel sauerbraten, or ragout.

10. Cheese souffle and potato It's a delicious accompaniment to goulash and stews.

11. Chanterelle dumplings They are delicious particularly when served when served with stews.

12. Dumpling Souffle Dumpling Souffle - A different kind of dumpling that pairs very good with stews.

13. Baked Gnocchi Cookies A essential side dish to try with stews. It's tasty.

14. Pallfy dumplings are a final type of dumpling is extremely delicious when cooked when served with stews.

Meat dishes

1. Greek stew made with Kritharaki

For 4 persons

Difficulty: Normal

Time to work: approx. 15 minutes

Time to produce Time of production: 1 hour and 45 minutes

Ingredients:

700 g of lamb of the leg or alternatively goulash of pork or beef

500 g beefsteak tomatoes or peeled tomatoes

200 grams of onions

200g of pasta (kritharaki)

3 . 3 cloves garlic

3 sprigs Thyme

2 tablespoons oil

1 tbsp tomato paste

1 teaspoon of paprika powder hot pink

Some cheese, parmesan

Salt and pepper

Preparation

1. Dry the meat and cut it into 3 centimeter-sized pieces. Slice the onion into pieces, and chop the garlic.

2. Cook the beefsteak tomatoes and add boiling water to them, and allow them to stand for 2 minutes. Rinse the tomatoes with cold water, then peel the tomatoes, then chop them into pieces.

3. Sear the meat into portions in a large pot. Sauté the garlic and onions. Make tomato paste by dissolving it in 250ml of hot water . Deglaze the onions and garlic

along with the tomatoes. Add the spices and cook for 5 minutes.

4. Put it in an oven-proof dish, cover with foil and cook for 1 hour at 225 degrees Celsius. Mix in the kritharaki as well as 750 ml of salted, boiling water and cook for an additional 30 minutes. Then, serve it with cheese grated.

2. Szeged goulash

For 4 persons

Difficulty: Normal

Time to work: approx. 20 minutes

Total production time 2 hours 20 minutes

Ingredients

800 g goulash, mixed

250 ml vegetable stock

150 ml of whipped, whipped cream 150 ml whipped

6 tbsp parsleychopped, 6 chopped

2 teaspoons of paprika powder noble sweet

2 teaspoons paprika powder hot pink

2 . teaspoons paste of tomatoes

Two teaspoons cumin powder

2 teaspoons dried oregano

One can sauerkraut

1 red pepper

1 bell pepper of yellow

1 onion

Salt and pepper

Preparation

1. Firsteaspoony chop finely the onions that are vegetable. Wash the peppers , then cut into pieces approximately one centimeter wide. Rinse off the sauerkraut. Mix the vegetables and the meat in the bowl of a large size. Add one teaspoon of sweet and hot paprika powder, two tablespoons of salt as well as 1 teaspoon caraway seeds and oregano, and pepper.

2. Preheat the oven at 190 ° and place the food into the roaster.

3. Bring the tomato paste, the cream and broth to a boiling point. Add salt and pepper, and pour the goulash mix. Cover the roaster with foil and cook in the oven for around 2 hours in the lower rack. Mix the goulash several times during cooking and cook for an additional 30 minutes, without lid.

4. Make sure to season the goulash towards the end. If required, sprinkle with

the caraway seeds, paprika powder as well as spice and salt. Sprinkle the parsley over prior to serving. Sour cream is a great complement to it.

3. Chicken and potatoes cooked in tomato sauce

For 2 persons

Difficulty: Normal

Time to work: approx. 30 minutes

Time to produce 1 hour 20 minutes

Ingredients

500 g potatoes

500ml of water

2 chicken legs

2 Tablespoons Olive Oil

1 onion

1 . Cubes of the broth

1 tbsp tomato paste

Salt and pepper

Basil

Paprika powder, noble sweet

Preparation

1. Peel, wash and cut the potatoes. Put the pieces in baking dish.

2. Peel and cut finely the onions. Fry in a pan using olive oil. Incorporate the tomato sauce, and sweat for a few minutes. Make a deglazing with water, then add the cube of stock. Add pepper, basil and plenty of salt. Bring the sauce up to the boiling point, then serve it on the potato.

3. Clean the legs of the chicken with water and dry. Sprinkle with paprika powder and salt. Put the legs on the top of the potatoes.

4. The oven should be heated to 200°C and cook for 45 minutes. Serve right away.

4. Veal cheeks

For 4 persons

Difficulty: Normal

Working time: approximately. 10 minutes

Time to produce 1 hour 55 min.

Ingredients

1 kg veal cheeks

400ml of red wine

350 ml veal stock

100g of celery

3 stems of Thyme

3 tablespoons olive oils

2 large carrots

2 meters. Parsley roots

1 Meter onion

1 Tbsp of flour

1 tbsp tomato paste

Salt and pepper

Preparation

1. Cleanse the vegetables, then chop in large chunks. Preheat the oven until 160°F.

2. Salt the meat and pepper. Cook the meat using hot oil the roasting pan of a large size. Remove the meat from the roaster and put it aside.

3. Roast the thyme as well as the vegetable in the saucepan. Sprinkle the flour over and then add to the tomatoes paste. Add the meat , and stir. Serve the red wine on top of the meat and bring to a boiling point. Add the broth, cover the pot

and simmer in the oven at a high temperature for 60 to 70 minutes.

4. The lid is removed and the stew can be cooked in the oven with the lid open for another 20-30 minutes. Reduce the liquid to a tiny spoonful and then remove the cheeks of veal. Let the liquid cool slightly.

5. The roast should be strained, then reduced the amount if required and season to taste. Take the tendons and any remaining fat off the roast. Serve the meat with the sauce. It is delicious with hazelnut spaetzle and frittered Hokkaido slices, and pretzel dumplings.

5. Pot of chicken and vegetables

For 2 persons

Difficulty: Easy

Time to work: approximately. 20 minutes

Time of production Time of production: 1 hour

Ingredients

500 G chicken breast fillets

500 ml clear soup

5 juniper berries

4 tbsp tomato paste

2 large onions

2cloves

2 carrots

2 small zucchini

1 leek stick

1 leaf of a bay

One piece of celeriac

1 pepper

Salt and pepper

Nutmeg and clove allspice, paprika powder oregano and rosemary the herb thyme

Preparation

1. Cut the ingredients into small pieces. Put everything into an oven-proof dish. Sprinkle the herb mixture generously.

2. Mix everything together well. Stir the hot stock with the paprika powder and tomato paste. Pour it over the other ingredients.

3. Preheat the oven at 200 degrees C. Let the stew simmer in the covered saucepan for around 60 minutes. In the last 30 mins, you can check whether there is enough liquid left in the pot and add more. If required, perform an assessment of the cooking at the end of 45 minutes.

4. The tomato paste, and the cooked onions result in a rich delicious sauce.

6. Stew pot schnitzel

For 4 persons

Difficulty: Easy

Time to work: approximately. 30 minutes

Total time of production: 2 hours 30 minutes

Ingredients

1 kg pork neck (forelock)

500ml red wine

200 ml vegetable stock

8 m.-sized potatoes

5 Juniper berries, pressed down

2 Meter onions

2 . 2 cloves garlic

2 tablespoons of the ketchup

1 Thyme sprig

1 rosemary sprig

1 teaspoon of sugar

1 tbsp of cranberries

Preparation

1. Cut the neck of the pork into thin slices of approximately 2.5 cm thick, then turn into flour.

2. Pour the oil in a pan and cook the meat in each of the sides. Sprinkle the meat with salt and place in a oven-safe casserole. Slice the onion into smaller pieces, then sweat in the pan until they turn golden yellow. Then add the sugar and cook the onions until tender. Add the juniper berries rosemary, garlic, a Thyme, a sprig, and ketchup. Deglaze by adding

red wine. Add salt to the sauce and then pour into the broth. Pour the sauce over the schnitzel.

3. The oven should be heated to 180 degrees C on top and bottom, then cook the schnitzel in the center rack 1.5 up to two hours.

4. Slice the potato as long as you can get them and add them after an hour, and cook at simultaneously. Add the cranberries to the mix and, if needed make the juice thicker by adding one teaspoon of starch.

7. Pork cheeks in beer sauce

For 4 persons

Difficulty: Easy

Time to work: approximately. 30 minutes

Total production time Time of production: 2 hours and 30 minutes

Ingredients

800 g pork cheek

300 G onions, roughly chopped

2 1/2 dl veal stock

2 Tablespoons Hot Mustard

2 Tbsp butter

1 . Slice of bread (wheat bread)

1/2 liter beer, dark

Salt and pepper

Bouquet garni

Preparation

1. In the meantime, melt butter the Dutch oven and cook onion in the oven.

2. Sprinkle salt and spice on the cheeks of the pork and cook the cheeks in a skillet until golden brown all over. Place the pork in the casserole.

3. The pan should be deglazed with beer and then remove any baked items off the base of the pot should they be required. Add the stock of veal and pour it over the steak. Add the bouquet Garni. Sprinkle the bread slice with mustard before placing it on the top. Cook on low heat for approximately two hours.

4. Remove the meat from the cooker then reduce the amount of sauce to a small amount if it is needed.

8. House style Burgundy meat

For 4 persons

Difficulty: Normal

Working time: approximately. 1 hour

Total production time 2 hours 30 minutes

Ingredients

1.2 kg of beef (shoulder or calves)

Red wine 750 ml (Pinot Noir) Dry

500 G shallots

250 ml beef , vegetable or beef stock

150g bacon, perfectly diced and smoke

4 large carrots

3 bay leaves

2 shallots, cut for the sauce

Two cloves of garlic

2 tablespoons of flour for sweating

2 tbsp tomato paste

One bunch of chopped parsley

Thyme

Salt and pepper

Preparation

1. Cut the meat into dices and fry into individual portions, then sprinkle salt and pepper. Set aside. Peel the shallots, cook them in bacon and one tablespoon of oil, and simmer for 10 minutes. Set aside.

2. Cut two carrots and two shallots into pieces and sauté along with garlic in a pan. Cook with 2 tablespoons of flour and stir in between. Then, deglaze the dish with beef stock, then pour in Pinot Noir and add tomato paste. Bring the mixture to a boil , then let it become thicker for a small spoon. Add salt, pepper, and thyme.

3. Place the meat, shallots along with Bay leaves, the sauce made with red wine, and some parsley stalks into a dish for baking. Then adjust the seasoning according to

taste. Cover and allow to simmer in the oven at the lowest rack, at 180 deg C for around one and a half hours.

4. To serve to serve, chop the remaining parsley, and sprinkle it on top of the meat. Spatzle as well. Pinot Noir are great together.

9. Veal the knuckle and knuckle with tomatoes white beans, and the lovage

For 4 persons

Difficulty: Normal

Time to work: approx. 15 minutes

Time to produce Time of production: 1 hour and 45 minutes

+

12 hours of sleep

Ingredients

250g of white beans dried

30 g butter lard

Ten cloves of fresh garlic

4 Calf shank

2 tablespoons loveage 2 tbsp lovage, chopped

One can of tomato

Black pepper and salt

Preparation

1. The beans should be soaked the day before. Bring the beans up to a boil using cold water. Then scrape the beans. Cover the pot with water and cook for approximately an hour at a low simmer.

2. Sprinkle salt and black pepper on the shanks of veal. Fry them on both sides in clarified butter that is hot. Remove the peels from the garlic cloves , then cut them in halves lengthwise. Add the toes to the meat , and cook for a few minutes.

3. Add the juice from tomato juice to meat. Sprinkle the lovage with a tablespoon on the meat. Cover and simmer on an even heat for approximately 90 minutes. Switch the heat off and continue to cook. If you need to you need to add 3-4 tablespoons of water once the gravy has sunk in on the surface of the saucepan.

4. About half an hour before cooking closes add the beans, and sprinkle with pepper and salt. Then add the tomatoes and season once more and sprinkle with remaining loveage. Baguette and risotto pair well together.

10. Turkey goulash comes from Westeros

For 4 persons

Difficulty: Normal

Time to work: approx. 20 minutes

Time to produce Time of production: 1 hour and 30 minutes

Ingredients

800 g of turkey goulash derived from the thigh

100ml red wine

Four teaspoons of spice

2 large onion vegetables

2 . 2 cloves garlic

2 Tbsp butter

2 tbsp honey

Two teaspoons of Majora

2 teaspoons of Thyme

Preparation

1. Make sure to use a casserole that is as large and as heavy as is possible. Get the meat out of the refrigerator to ensure that it is at the temperature of room.

2. Peel the onions, then cut into small cubes. remove the garlic.

3. Cook the cookware over medium-high heat. Add the butter until it starts to foam. Add the onion cubes, and mix throughout. Add the honey, and allow the onions to caramelize until they are light brown, stirring often. Press the garlic and add it to the pan sweat, then and spices mix to onions. Incorporate everything and then pour into the red wine.

4. Incorporate the meat until it's a little bit seared. Lower the heat stirring and adding an ounce of salt. If there isn't enough liquid to cover the dish, add a couple of teaspoons of liquid. Cover the pot and let it simmer for 45 to 60 minutes. Mix every now and again Add more liquid, if necessary.

5. Once the meat is cooked you can cover it in water Bring to a boiling point and then make the sauce thicker. Switch off the stove add more seasoning and let it simmer for another 10 minutes. Serve, as a side dish , spaetzle, farmer's bread dumplings, red cabbage and salad.

11. Peperonata with salsiccia

For 4 persons

Difficulty: Normal

Working time: approximately. 25 minutes

Total production time 45 minutes

Ingredients

350 grams salsiccia

100 g of tomatoes that have been dried

100 black golives

100ml red wine

100 ml vegetable stock

3 toes garlic

2 peppers, yellow

2 red peppers

2 onions

2 hot peppers

2 tbsp balsamic vinegar

Two teaspoons capers

1 baguette

1 spring onion

1 lemon

1 rosemary sprig

1 packet Gnocchi fresh, approx. 600 g

1 . Can of tomato separated, 500 grams

Paprika powder

sugar

Salt and pepper

Preparation

1. The salsiccia in thin strips. Get rid of the seeds in the peppers before cutting them into strips. Slice the tomato into long strips. Remove the olives' stones to cut the olives into pieces. Chop the rosemary and garlic extremely small. Grate and squeeze the lemon. Cut the onions into dices and

cut spring onions in rings. Chop the pepperoni as well as the parmesan cheese.

2. Cook your salsiccia in a small amount of oil. Add the garlic, chili and rosemary. Make sure to sear it thoroughly so that the sausage doesn't escape from the skin. Lower the heat and cook the onions for 2 to three minutes, so that they begin to become sweet.

3. Increase the heat and add the pepper slices and cook for 2 up to 3 minutes. Make a glaze using balsamic vinegar wine and stock. Add the tomatoes juice, lemon zest and lemon juice. Mix briefly before adding the other ingredients, with the exception for the spring onions and parmesan.

4. Season with freshly ground black pepper sea salt powder, paprika and some sugar. Bring to a boil and then reduce heat to simmer for 10 minutes. Cover the

baking paper with the pan and let it simmer at a simmer for about 20 minutes. Continue to push away air bubbles.

5. When the cooking time is over make sure to heat your butter over a saucepan and cook the gnocchi for 5 to 7 minutes.

6. The baking parchment is removed from the sauce, and add the spring onions and parmesan in the dish. Stir well and serve.

12. Fiery Turmeric Chicken

For 4 persons

Difficulty: Normal

Working time: approximately. 20 minutes

Time to produce 1 hour 50 minutes

Ingredients

400 g vine tomatoes

300 G shallots

60ml water

50 g rock mushrooms, dried

4 chicken legs, skinless

Three tablespoons of olive oil 3 tablespoons rapeseed oil

3 drops of lemon juice

1 1/2 tsp turmeric

1 carrot

1 tablespoon oil from the pepper

1 tablespoon Sour cream

1 teaspoon of sugar

1 bunch of chopped parsley

Salt and pepper

Cayenne pepper or chili pepper

Preparation

1. Remove the stalks from the tomatoes, chop shallots, then cut the legs of the chicken at the joint. Pour around 60 ml of boiling water in a glass and add dried mushroom.

2. In the roaster, sprinkle the pieces of leg with salt and black pepper, fry until golden brown. Then take them out of the pan. Cook the onion until they are translucent. Slice the carrot in thin pieces, then add the turmeric powder and cook in a short time while stirring. Chop and soak the mushrooms, then add the water from the mushrooms that has been filtered. Put the water of the mushrooms into the tea filter and then filter it. Add the tomatoes as well as the legs into the pot too. The tomatoes are seasoned prior to cooking with salt, pepper, and sugar according to your preference. Let the tomatoes simmer covered for approximately 1 hour and 15 minutes.

3. Serve with a few drops of fresh lemon juice as well as chopped chopped parsley. To finish with a teaspoon of Sour cream, if you need it add chili peppers and cayenne peppers. Basmati or flatbread, or Tagliatelle are great with it.

13. Krumeltiger Braised Galinha

For 2 persons

Difficulty: Normal

Working time: approximately. 20 minutes

Time to produce 1 hour 20 minutes

Ingredients

800g can tomatoes peeled

500 g chicken legs

6 large onions

3 toes garlic

1 tablespoon olive oil 1 tablespoon olive

1 teaspoon dried oregano

Salt and pepper

Preparation

1. Peel the onions and garlic. Don't slice the garlic or onions into tiny cubes. Divide the onions in half, then cut into thin slices of one centimeter in thickness. The chickpeas are then drained through an ice-cold strainer.

2. The oil should be heated in the saute pan. Fry the chicken legs, turning them over on both sides. Add the chickpeas, garlic oregano, tomatoes and the liquid, and a little salt. Bring the entire mixture to a simmer. Put the chicken pieces into the pan, skin side down. Cover the pan and cook at a low temperature for 50-60

minutes. Sprinkle with salt and pepper towards the at the end.

3. Serve with pasta or potatoes.

14. Lamb curry, yogurt and spinach

For 4 persons

Difficulty: Normal

Time to work: approximately. 30 minutes

Total time to produce: 50 minutes

Ingredients

600 g spinach leaves

400 grams of Lamb (leg or loin)

200 g of natural yogurt

15 ginger

4 onions

2 . 2 cloves garlic

2 tablespoons oil

Ground cumin 1 tablespoon

1 teaspoon turmeric

1 teaspoon coriander

1 teaspoon cardamom

1/2 TEASPOON Chili powder

1/2 TSP of fenugreek

1/4 TEASPOON Cayenne pepper

salt

Preparation

1. Clean the spinach that you have picked and take out the tough stalks. Place the spinach in the bowl then sprinkle boiling water over it and allow it to sit for a short time. Rinse the spinach in a colander under cold water and then drain. Rinse the

meat, dry, then cut into smaller pieces. Peel the onions and garlic and cut them into thin slices. Peel the ginger, then grate it into a fine grate.

2. In an oven and fry in the onion while mixing. Add the meat, garlic , and ginger and sauté until everything is brown. Add the spices and cook for a few minutes. Add 300 ml of water then cover with a lid and simmer for 20 minutes, stirring regularly. Then add the spinach, and simmer for an additional 10 minutes. Then allow the sauce to boil at a high temperature for 5 minutes. Mix the yoghurt until it is creamy and then stir it in the curry, and season using salt and heat but don't bring it up to a simmer. Place the remaining yogurt over the curry.

3. Basmati rice is a great match for it.

15. Kasseler goulash made of white cabbage

For 2 persons

Difficulty: Normal

Time to work: approx. 25 minutes

Time of production 1 hour and 5 minutes

Ingredients

500 g Kasseler

500 g of white cabbage cut into strips

500ml of water

4 juniper berries

4 . Four grain of allspice

1onion, cut into fine strips

1/2 tbsp honey

1/2 ELCreme fraiche

1/2 teaspoon of broth Instant

Salt and pepper

Tomato paste

Preparation

1. Cut the cabbage and onion into thin strips. Do not slice the meat too small.

2. Warm the clarified butter, and cook the cubes of meat for 7 to 8 minutes. After five minutes, add tomato paste as well as the onion strips. Dissolve the water in the deglazing, then cut white cabbage into pieces and add to the pot. Add the spices, and the powdered broth and simmer for approximately 40 minutes.

3. The goulash should be seasoned with honey, salt, and pepper and then mix into the crème fraiche.

4. This can be eaten with jacket potatoes or boiling potatoes.

16. Lamb pot

For 6 persons

Difficulty: Easy

Time of work: approximately. 1 hour

Total production time Time of production: 3 hours 30 minutes

Ingredients:

1 1/2 kilograms of bones-free lamb legs

1 1/2 kg potatoes

1.5 kg of carrots

4 bay leaves

Three cloves of garlic

1 vegetable onion

One bunch of Thyme

3/4 liters of vegetable stock

1/2 Liter red wine

Herbs to garnish

Oil to fry

Salt and pepper

Preparation

1. Cut the meat into small pieces. Peel the garlic and onions. Chop the garlic , and chop the onions. Chop the carrots, then chop the potato into thin slices.

2. The meat is fried in pieces and then season it by adding salt and pepper. Put the entire meat in the roaster. Add the onions and garlic and cook for about a minute. Place the potato slices over the carrots. Season them with salt and pepper.

3. Spread the bay leaves over the top. Then, mix in the wine and wine. Cover and cook in the oven that has been preheated

for approximately 2.5 hour at 175 degrees C. Sprinkle with the herbs before serving.

17. Double cooked and seasoned beef

For 6 persons

Difficulty: Normal

The working time is approximately. 30 minutes

Time to produce Total production time: 3 hours 55 mins

Ingredients

1kg beef (beef rump)

120 ml soy sauce, light

Six slices of ginger

4 toes garlic

4 Dry or red wine

3star anise

3 shallots

3 Peanut Oil

3 tbsp soy sauce, dark

2 mandarins, peel, dried

2 tbsp bean sauce

2 tablespoons of Szechuan chili pepper

Two teaspoons of cornstarch

1 teaspoon of sugar

1 tablespoon sesame oil

Salt and pepper

Preparation

1. First cut the rump of beef into thin slices along the grain, then cut into pieces. In the peanut oil, heat a pan , and fry the beef pieces on both sides. Remove the meat from the pan and place it aside.

2. Remove the majority of the oil and cook in the Szechuan peppers, shallots garlic, mandarin peel aniseed and ginger for a couple of minutes. Mix it up again and again. Add the two soy sauces as well as the sherry, and cook for five more minutes.

3. The water should be heated until the base sauce is dissolved. Utilizing a spoon with a slotted handle, get rid of the spices and dispose of them. Add the beef cubes, bean sauce cubes, and sugar to the sauce, and fill up with water until the meat is fully covered. Bring the sauce to a boil, then let it simmer, covered, on an extremely low heat for 3 hours.

4. Salt and pepper. Mix the starch with a small amount of cold water, and make use of it to make the sauce thicker. Sprinkle with sesame oil and serve.

18. Slices of Rustic Beef Leg

For 6 persons

Difficulty: Normal

Time to work: approx. 45 minutes

Production time total: four hrs 10 minutes

Ingredients

250 G carrots

250 g of celery

250ml port wine

6 m.-large beef leg discs

5m. Onions

3 toes garlic

2 tbsp tomato paste

2 tbsp mustard, medium hot

2 tbsp tomato paste

1 Liter beef broth

Additionally

20 peppercorns of small size that are crushed

5 small allspice grain, crushed

Two bay leaves cut up

1 teaspoon of majoran dried

1 teaspoon rosemary dried

Preparation

1. Wash the steak slices thoroughly, removing bone fragments, and wipe dry. Clean the garlic, vegetables and onions, and cut them into smaller pieces. Preheat the oven at 240 degrees C. Then, heat a casserole over the hotplate at the highest setting for heat.

2. Cook the leg slices inside the dish until they begin to change hue. Take them out and place in a bowl covered. After that, add the veggies and cook them. Then, add the spice mix paprika powder as well as tomato paste and mustard and cook until the vegetables have formed roasting substances.

3. Then, deglaze the dish using the wine. When the wine is reduced completely then continue to sweat it then place the slices of leg on top of the vegetable bed and then deglaze the dish by adding broth. Place the casserole into the oven and bake it at 240 degrees C in 20 mins. Then keep it covered for 30 minutes at 170 degrees C. After that allow the slices of beef to rest on the plate for 5 minutes.

4. Take the liquid through a strainer, put it in a bowl, and then season according to your the desired taste.

Vegetarian dishes

1. Cabbage Roulade with bulgur filling

For 4 persons

Difficulty: Easy

Time to work: approximately. 45 minutes

Time to produce 1 hour 30 minutes

Ingredients

600 ml vegetable stock

150 g bulgur

150 g of skinned and roasted peppers

100 grams of feta

100 G double cream cheese

50ml of whipped cream

8 large white cabbage leaves

6 Tbsp oil

3 Tbsp light sauce thickener

2 eggs (size M)

2 teaspoons of oregano (dried)

1 onion

1 . A clove

Salt and pepper

Preparation

1. Cut the onion and garlic into small pieces and sauté in 2 tablespoons of oil heated until the onion is translucent. Then add the bulgur, and sauté briefly. Bring the soup to a boil, adding 300 ml of stock. Cook covered for 10 minutes on an unrefined temperature.

2. Rinse the bell peppers and rub dry and cut into pieces. The feta is crumbled in a

large chunk and add it to the bulgur, along with the egg, cream cheese, and bell pepper. Mix the mixture with pepper, oregano and salt until you have a consistent mixture.

3. The cabbage leaves should be cooked in salted boiling water for 3 minutes. Then, let them cool, then shake off and dry. The leaf veins should be cut in a flat fashion and put two to three tablespoons of bulgur on top of leaf. Place the edges of the leaves over it. Then, roll from the bottom of the stalk until the top side of the leaf. Secure with kitchen thread.

4. Cook the roulades on pans with 4 tablespoons oil, evenly spread across the sides. Pour in 300 ml stock, bring to a boil, cover , and cook on medium heat over 45 minutes. Take the roulades out of the broth. Add the cream and bind by adding the thickener to the sauce and pepper, then add salt.

2. Pumpkin curry and mango

For 4 persons

Difficulty: Normal

Working time: approximately. 45 minutes

Time to produce Time of production: 1 hour and 10 minutes

Ingredients

Garam Masala

6 black peppercorns

4 cloves

3 cardamom pods

1 leaf from a bay

1 tablespoon coriander seeds

1 teaspoon turmeric

1/4 cinnamon stick

1 teaspoon Cumin Seeds

stew

1 kg Butternut Squash

400 ml coconut milk

200 g green beans

50 g cashew nuts

20 g ginger

6 stems coriander green

3 tablespoons lemon juice

2 onions

1 . A clove

1 mango

1 tbsp butter lard

Salt and pepper

Preparation

1. crush the cardamom pods to make Garam Masala. Garam Masala, remove the stones. Roast the pods as well as additional spices inside a saucepan until they smell delicious. Finely pound them in a Moser and put aside.

2. Clean the beans before making the stew, slice into pieces that are about 4 centimeters wide and simmer in salted boiling water for 2 minutes. Then drain and then cool down using ice water. Cut the cashew nuts in pieces.

3. Finely chop the onions and garlic. Peel the ginger and chop it finely. Peel and cut the pumpkin in half and remove the seeds using the help of a spoon. Slice the pumpkin into 2 cubes. Remove the mango's peel to cut into cubes of about one centimeter wide.

4. The clarified butter is heated in an oven. Saute the garlic, ginger as well as onions. Add cashew nuts , garam masala. Toast briefly. Add the pumpkin and mango cubes. Deglaze the dish using 300 ml of water as well as coconut milk. Cover and cook on an even heat for 10 minutes. Bring the beans to a simmer and add lemon juice salt and pepper. The coriander leaves should be removed from the stems, and then sprinkle them on the curry.

3. Chili sin carne

For 4 persons

Difficulty: Easy

Time to work: approximately. 65 minutes

Total time of production: 65 minutes

Ingredients

215 G halloumi cheese

100 grams of carrots

100 grams of leek

100 g celeriac

6 tbsp olive oil

2 pieces of tomatoes

2 chilis red

1 teaspoon of cumin

1 . A bunch of spring onions

1 vegetable onion

1 red pepper

One clove of garlic

1 yellow pepper

1 kidney bean

1 tbsp rose hot powder of paprika

1/4 teaspoon of black cumin

sugar

Salt and pepper

Preparation

1. Peel the carrots and celery. Clean the leeks and then cut the vegetables into small pieces. Finely dice onion and garlic. Clean the peppers, and remove the seeds. The pods can be cut into two centimeter-sized pieces. Cut the chili peppers in half lengthwise, then remove the seeds, and then slice them into pieces.

2. Three tablespoons of oil are heated in the casserole. Saute the onions and garlic until they are translucent. Add the chili as well as the rest of the veggies and cook all over. Sprinkle cumin and paprika over the top, and toast lightly. Pour 100ml of boiling water on top. Add tomatoes, and cook covered for 20 minutes.

3. Wash the kidney beans with a colander , then drain them. Place the beans in the pan, bring to a boil. Season with salt, pepper and sugar.

4. Clean the spring onions , and cut into rings that are fine Then sprinkle the chili. Cleanse the halloumi, dry it, then cut into pieces that are one centimeter thick. Cook halloumi in the remaining oil each side until it is golden on the outside. Serve with cumin and black pepper, and serve the chili with it.

4. Cheese dumplings and bread on red and beetroot

For 4 persons

Difficulty: Normal

Working time: approximately. 45 minutes

Time to produce 1 hour and 35 minutes

Ingredients:

Beetroot cabbage red

Red cabbage 900g

250 ml vegetable stock

200 milliliters port wine 200 ml

3 Tbsp red wine vinegar

2 shallots

2 bay leaves

2 red prayers

1 tbsp butter lard

1 cup allspice (ground)

Salt and pepper

Cheese dumplings and bread

200 ml milk

200 g strong Tyrolean mountain cheese

80 grams of butter

25 G pine nuts

15 juniper berries

6 rolls of the previous day

2 eggs (size M)

2 shallots

1 egg yolk (size M)

1 Tbsp clarified butter

1/2 teaspoon cumin seeds

1 teaspoon coriander seeds

Salt and pepper

Preparation

1. Cleanse the cabbage and split into four parts, and then remove the stalk. Cut the quarters into strips of thin. Finely chop

shallots. Cook 1 teaspoon of clarified butter to a high pan and sauté shallots until they become translucent. Then add the cabbage, and cook for 5 minutes, stirring frequently. Peel and finely grate the beetroot. The bay leaves, the allspice, and beetroot in the cabbage, add salt and pepper to taste. Include the vinegar, stock along with port wine. Place the lid on the pan and heat it to the temperature of boiling. Cook on a moderate simmer for about an hour and 15 minutes.

2. Slice the roll into small pieces. Place them in a shallow bowl. Crush the caraway and coriander seeds with a mortar, then add them to the rolls. Finely chop shallots. In a saucepan, heat a tablespoon of clarified butter, and fry shallots until translucent. Remove the pan from the heat source. Mix in the eggs, milk, and egg yolks. Add plenty of salt and pepper and pour it over the bread rolls.

3. Bring plenty of water to a boiling point in a large pot and then sprinkle it using plenty of salt. Cut the cheese of mountain into half centimeter chunks. The bread rolls should be kneaded using your hand, then knead it into the cheese. Wet your hands form 18 dumplings approximately the size of an average table tennis ball from the dough. Place them in the boiling water, and let it the mixture simmer for around 20 minutes at moderate temperature.

4. Crush the juniper berries in a mortar. Then, fry them in butter on medium temperature to golden. Mix in the juniper fruits and take them off the heat. Remove the dumplings from the water using an elongated spoon. Remove the dumplings to kitchen paper. If you want, season the red and beetroot by adding salt and black pepper. Place the dumplings over the top of the pine nuts and the juniper butter.

5. Veggie Bolo

For 6 persons

Difficulty: Easy

The working time is approx. 55 minutes

Time to produce Time of production: 1 hour and 20 minutes

Ingredients

500 grams of mushrooms

500 g spaghetti

100 hard Italian cheeses

Four stems of Thyme

4 Tbsp oil

Three cloves of garlic

2 cans tomatoes

2 carrots

2 stalks of celeria

2 bay leaves

1 vegetable onion

1 rosemary sprig

1 tbsp tomato paste

1 teaspoon sweet powder of paprika

1 teaspoon of sugar

Salt and pepper

Preparation

1. Clean and chop your mixed mushroom. Preheat the oven at 50 °. Place the mushrooms out on an oven sheet. Dry on the middle rack for 30 minutes.

2. Peel the carrots and wash the celery. Finely chop the onion and carrots, and celery. Cut a clove garlic.

3. The oil should be heated in a separate saucepan and roast the mushrooms on an extremely high heat. Add the onions and the vegetables and cook on a moderate heat for about four minutes. Slice two garlic cloves in thin slices and then add. Incorporate 2 bay leaves. Finely chop rosemary and thyme, and mix with the bay leaves. Add tomato paste, tomatoes peeled and then crush them into a fine powder. Add 400 ml of water. Season with sugar, paprika powder and salt. Bring the water to a boil and simmer on moderate heat for about 25 minutes.

4. Take plenty of water salted to a boil , then cook the spaghetti until it is al al dente. Drain, and then mix the sauce. Serve with cheese that is hard.

6. Ratatouille

For 6 persons

Difficulty: Normal

Time to work: approx. 35 minutes

Time to produce Time of production: 1 hour and 20 minutes

Ingredients

750 g zucchini

700 g tomatoes (medium-sized)

500 g vegetable onions

6 tbsp olive oil

5 cloves garlic

4 rosemary sprigs

1Yellow pepper

1 red pepper

1 eggplant

One bunch of Thyme

Salt and pepper

Preparation

1. The onions are cut into four parts, and then slice them into thin strips. The garlic is cut into strips. Peel the eggplant, then cut it into four slices. Cut them into pieces of three centimeters long and then into 1 centimeter-thick sticks. Dab with the hot peppers. rinse and cut into four centimeter-long pieces. Clean the zucchini, then cut into 1 centimeter wide slices.

2. Two tablespoons of oil are heated in a large skillet. Cook the onions and garlic in them on an open flame until they become translucent. Preheat the oven at 180 ° and continue to cook onions and garlic in an ovenproof dish large enough to last for 10 minutes on the bottom rack.

3. 2 tablespoons of oil in a pot. Grill the eggplants and peppers on a medium-low temperature for 5 minutes before changing. Put them into the mold. Two

teaspoons of olive oil then fry up the zucchini. Pick the rosemary and thyme , then chop. In the zucchini, add the tin. Add pepper and salt.

4. Cut the tomatoes along the round side , then place into boiling water to cook for brief duration. Peel, quench and cut into half. Take off the stem end. Mix the tomatoes and the vegetables and stew for about 45 minutes, and season with salt and pepper.

7. Mushroom stew

For 4 persons

Difficulty: Easy

Time to work: approximately. 20 minutes

Production time total 1 hour

Ingredients

800 g of mushrooms

200 g of wheat flour

100 g of wholemeal rye flour

50g Parmesan grated

Port wine 50ml

50ml white wine

15 G dried stone mushrooms

The majora has 10 stems.

Ten tablespoons of olive oil

2 rosemary sprigs

Two cloves of garlic

2 ELESSig

1 leek stick

1 Tbsp butter

Half a bunch of fresh parsley

1 bunch of chives

Half a cube (or 12 cup) of yeast

1/4 teaspoon salt

Preparation

1. Mix wheat flour with wholemeal rye into the bowl. Create a hole in the middle and then crush your yeast in it. Add 150 ml water, 2 tablespoons of olive oil, and salt. Mix everything together into a soft dough. Knead with the parmesan.

2. Cleaning and washing the leeks. Then , cut it into narrow rings. After thoroughly cleaning the mushrooms, chop them roughly and then put them in a casserole that is oven-safe. Add garlic cloves, leeks dried porcini mushrooms as well as four stalks of marjoram and rosemary. Season with a pinch of salt. Add the butter, port as well as white wine, water, and the port and cover.

3. Preheat the oven until 200°F. The dough is then kneaded again, and form it into a large roll. Put the dough on the edges of the lid. It will help seal the pot with airtight. Bring the water to a boil over high temperature. Then, cook in the middle of the stove for 40 minutes.

4. Take the leaves from the parsley, and the six marjoram stalks, and chop them finely. Chop the chives up into small rolls. Mix them with eight tablespoons olive oil and between one and two tablespoons of vinegar. Season with salt.

5. When you have finished the cooking time, gently remove the edges of the bread crust. Add salt and pepper to the stew with the mushrooms, and serve it with the herb oil and bread crust.

8. Gritinated eggplant

For 2 persons

Difficulty: Easy

The working time is approximately. 20 minutes

Total production time 5 hours

Ingredients

500 geggplants

100 g creme fraiche

50 Italian hard cheese (grated)

6 tbsp olive oil

One can of tomato sauce

1 . A clove

1 . A pinch or two of cayenne pepper

1/2 bunch flat-leaf parsley

sugar

Salt and pepper

Preparation

1. Clean the eggplant and cut into half-a-centimeter-thick slices. Make sure to grease a tray with 1 spoonful of oil. Add salt and pepper to both of the slices of eggplant and arrange them side-by-side onto the baking sheet. Sprinkle with 2 teaspoons of olive oil. The oven should be heated to 200 degrees , then roast the eggplants over the middle rack for 30 to 35 mins.

2. Take the parsley leaves off the stems and chop them up roughly. Blend the tomato pizzas with the garlic clove that has been crushed and half the parsley, and one tablespoon of oil. Sprinkle with cayenne pepper as well as the sugar salt and pepper. Mix the cheese and the crème fraiche.

3. Make sure to grease a baking dish with oil, about a tablespoon. Layer the slices of eggplant and tomato sauce on top of the

pan. Sprinkle the creme fraiche cheese mixture over the top.

4. Pre-heat the oven up to 200 degrees. Bake the eggplants placed on the rack in the middle for about 15 minutes, until they're golden brown. Sprinkle the remaining parsley over the top and serve.

9. Artichoke pan

For 2 persons

Difficulty: Easy

The working time is approximately. 25 minutes

Time of production 1 hour

Ingredients

200 g potatoes

150 g of king oyster mushrooms

150 ml vegetable stock

100ml white wine

Four artichokes in small pieces

2 red onions

2 tablespoons of parsley (chopped)

Two tablespoons of olive oil

1 . A clove

1 red pepper

1 cup of lemon peel (finely grated)

Salt and pepper

Preparation

1. Pick the leaves of the artichoke to reveal tender yellow leaves, then cut off the stems. Split the artichokes by dividing the stalk into two pieces. Scrape the hay away using one teaspoon. Divide the two halves by cutting the leaves into small pieces.

2. Peel and cut into pieces the potato. Cut the garlic with a squeezing motion, then cut the onions into strips , and sauté with the artichokes as well as the potatoes in hot oil. Then, deglaze the pan with stock and wine and cook covered for between 25 and 35 minutes.

3. Slice the bell peppers into rings, and the mushrooms into smaller pieces. Cook each for about 10 minutes. Serving with pepper and salt, and garnished with lemon and parsley zest.

10. Cabbage rolls with risotto and mushrooms filling

For 2 persons

Difficulty: Easy

Time to work: approximately. 55 minutes

Time to produce 1 hour 30 minutes

Ingredients

300g of mushrooms (small)

200 g risotto rice

150ml white wine

12 large white cabbage leaves

4 Tbsp oil

3 tablespoons parsley (chopped)

1 Liter of porcini mushroom broth that is hot

1/2 1 TEASPOON chili flakes

salt

Preparation

1. The salted and salted waters to a boiling point and then boil in the leaves of cabbage for 3 minutes. Drain, then squish and wipe dry. Remove the leaf veins. Bring

600 ml of water to a simmer, add rice Cover and cook over the stove at a low temperature for 15 minutes.

2. Remove the dried mushrooms. Cut 200 grams of mushrooms in half. Place two tablespoons of oil into a roasting pan coated with oil and cook them until they are golden. add salt. Mix in the rice and add the chili flakes and chopped parsley. Finely chop the rest of the mushrooms.

3. Place 2 to 3 tablespoons of mushroom risotto onto each leaf of cabbage. Then fold the edges of the sides over and then wrap the ends of the stalk up. Secure the stalk with kitchen thread.

4. Chop the mushrooms and fry them in the fat of the fryer to golden-brown. Pour into the wine and reduce it to half. Add the roulades along with 400 milliliters of boiling stock. Cover, bring to a simmer for 20 minutes.

5. The roulades should be kept warm. Puree the sauce to a fine consistency. Serve it with the Roulades.

11. Curry and stew of vegetables

For 6 persons

Difficulty: Easy

Time to work: approximately. 20 minutes

Total production time 45 minutes

Ingredients

800 ml vegetable stock

500 g potatoes

250 G carrots

250 grams of leek

150 g of yogurt made from whole milk

100 g of sour-cream

4 tbsp of parsley (chopped)

3 tablespoons oil

3 TBSP mild curry powder

2 onions

2 . 2 cloves garlic

1 small cauliflower

1 2 tbsp lemon juice

1 Tbsp of flour

1/2 teaspoon cumin (ground)

1 teaspoon of sugar

Chili powder

Salt and pepper

Preparation

1. Cut the carrots them in half lengthways
, then break into smaller pieces. Clean the

cauliflower and cut into tiny florets. Wash and clean the leeks. The light and dark greens are cut into rings. Peel the potatoes and cut them into pieces.

2. Cut the garlic into small pieces and onions. In a large pot and cook the vegetables. Add the onions and garlic and sauté briefly. In a small skillet, toast 2 teaspoons of curry. Add broth to the deglazing, then add chili pepper, salt and chili. Mix the flour with sour cream, then add it to the stew and bring it to the point of boiling. Cover and cook on moderate temperature for 15 to 20 mins.

3. Mix the yogurt with one teaspoon chili, one tablespoon cumin 2 tablespoons parsley salt, pepper lemon juice, and one teaspoon of sugar. Add remaining curry, salt, pepper, and curry. Sprinkle it with 2 tablespoons of parsley , and serve alongside yogurt dip.

12. Veggie goulash

For 2 persons

Difficulty: Normal

Time to work: approximately. 30 minutes

Total production time: 40 mins

Ingredients

250 g seitan

200 ml vegetable stock

100 G onions

2 tablespoons parsley (chopped)

2 tablespoons oil

2 tablespoons paprika pulp

2 teaspoons rose-hot powder of paprika

1 yellow pepper

1 zucchini (small)

1 . A clove

1 teaspoon cumin seeds

sugar

Salt and pepper

Preparation

1. Cut the garlic clove into small pieces and onions. Clean and clean the peppers and zucchini. Cut into cubes that are about one inch wide. Heat oil in a saucepan. Sauté with paprika, garlic onions and zucchini in it. Then, cook the caraway seeds as well as the paprika pulp, paprika seeds and paprik powder.

2. In the end, deglaze the pot with vegetable stock and sprinkle with salt, pepper and sugar, add a pinch and salt. Cover and cook on medium-low temperature. The seitan is cut into cubes of about 2 centimeters in size. Add them to the goulash, and cook open for 10

minutes. Adjust seasoning if needed and garnish with parsley.

13. The pumpkin risotto is topped with walnuts

For 2 persons

Difficulty: Normal

Time to work: approx. 15 minutes

Total time to produce: 40 minutes

Ingredients

600 ml vegetable stock

400 g Hokkaido pumpkin

150 g risotto rice

100ml white wine

50 g parmesan

5 stalks parsley

5 Tbsp oil

2 tablespoons walnut kernels

1 onion

1 Tbsp butter

Salt and pepper

Preparation

1. Cut the onion into pieces. Clean the pumpkin, and then remove seeds with the help of an utensil. Cut the pulp that is not peeled in 1.5 centimeter squares. The broth should be heated in a pot and then keep it warm.

2. A tablespoon of butter and oil in a separate saucepan. Cook the onion cubes in the steamer until they become translucent. Add pumpkin and rice, and cook for 2 minutes. Then, deglaze the dish with white wine and allow it to boil to a

complete boil. Pour the broth over the rice. Cook on a medium-low temperature for about 25 minutes, making sure to stir it every now and then. Add the stock slowly until it's nearly soaked through the rice.

3. Pick the parsley off the stalk, then chop. Chop the walnuts, and mix them with four tablespoons oil and the parsley.

4. Sprinkle salt on the risotto , then mix in the cheese. Pour the walnut oil and parsley oil over it, and serve.

14. Braised onions

For 2 persons

Difficulty: Normal

Working time: approximately. 10 minutes

Total production time Time of production: 30 minutes

Ingredients

700 g vegetable onions

White wine 125 ml 125 ml

30 g sultanas

25 g tomatoes (dried)

3 stems of Thyme

2 bay leaves

2 Tablespoons of Sugar

Two tablespoons of olive oil

2 tablespoons dark-beet syrup

Preparation

1. The vegetable's roots onions must remain. Peel and then cut the onions. The onion half is cut in slices. Slice the dried tomatoes into small pieces.

2. In the meantime, heat the olive oil in a pan , and then fry onions on medium heat until they are golden brown. Sprinkle

sugar over them and let it begin to caramelize.

3. Pour white wine into a saucepan, then and add beet syrup, bay leaves the thyme, sultanas and diced tomatoes. Cover and simmer on the medium heat for about 20 minutes.

15. Mini paks with braised choy

For 10 people

Difficulty: Normal

Time to work: approximately. 10 minutes

Total time of production: 30 minutes

Ingredients

150 ml chicken broth

100 grams of shiitake mushroom

5 mini paks Choy

4 tablespoons oil

3 tbsp rice wine

2 tbsp light soy sauce

1 red pepper

1 teaspoon cornstarch

Preparation

1. The pak choy is divided lengthways. The pepper is cut in half lengthways. take out the seeds and cut the pepper diagonally in thin pieces. Clean the shiitake mushroom.

2. In the wok. Then, fry the mushrooms and the peppers in it for about two or three minutes. Serve with rice wine, chicken stock as well as soy sauce. Include the pak choy. the cut side is on the bottom. Cover and cook on medium heat for three or four minutes.

3. Mix 4 tablespoons of water and starch. Bring the mixture to a boiling point, then thicken it with starch and pour it over the pakchoy and serve.

16. Goulash made of cucumber and mushrooms

For 4 persons

Difficulty: Normal

Working time: approximately. 10 minutes

Total production time Time of production: 30 minutes

Ingredients

White mushrooms of 500 grams

300g brown mushroom

250 g sour cream

150 g King oyster mushrooms

150 g chanterelles

175 ml dry white wine

30 grams butter

3 onions

2 tablespoons oil

1 cucumber

1 . A clove

1 Tbsp finely chopped dill

1 tablespoon 1 teaspoon lemon peel (finely grated)

White pepper and salt

Preparation

1. Cut the onion into small pieces. Chop the garlic finely and mix it with lemon zest. Clean the mushrooms, then cut the larger ones into half. Peel the cucumber, then

cut it lengthwise. Take out the seeds and slice into two centimeters pieces.

2. Butter and oil in a skillet. Cook the mushrooms in a few portions before putting them aside. Then add onions cubes into the skillet and cook until they are light brown. Pour into the white wine Bring to a boiling and add the mushrooms to the pan.

3. Incorporate sour cream, and stir into. Cover and cook the mushrooms on a medium temperature for 12 minutes. Add the pieces of cucumber and the garlic-lemon mix after 5 minutes. Add the dill to the mix at the end of cooking time. Then, season it by adding the salt as well as pepper. Spaetzle is a great accompaniment.

17. Orange Savoy cabbage

For 2 persons

Difficulty: Easy

Time to work: approximately. 10 minutes

Total production time: 30 mins

Ingredients

400 g savoy , a savoy cabbage

3 ELCreme fraiche

2 TBSP butter

1 orange

1 organic orange

Preparation

1. The savoy cabbage should be cut in pieces. Rub the skin from the orange

organically lightly. squeeze the juice. Peel the orange in a thick layer and then slice the orange flesh.

2. Warm the butter in a non-stick skillet. Savoy cabbage is cooked throughout. Add two spoons of peel of an orange the salt, and the pepper. Add the juice of an orange. Stew covered for 8 to 10 minutes. Blend the cream fraiche in a bowl and add it to the savoy cabbage as well as those orange pieces. Serve immediately after a brief heating.

18. Baked paprika vegetable

For 2 persons

Difficulty: Easy

Time to work: approximately. 20 minutes

Total production time 30-minute production time

Ingredients

100 g creme fraiche

100 g of feta

Three tablespoons of olive oil

2tomatoes

1 red pepper

1 green pepper

1 yellow pepper

1 zucchini

One clove of garlic

1 white onion

1 leaf of a bay

Salt and pepper

Preparation

1. Clean and chop the peppers roughly. Slice the zucchini into half, then cut into long slices. Cut tomatoes into small pieces. Cut the onions in half , and then cut them into pieces. Cut the clove of garlic into small cubes.

2. In a pan, heat oil and cook onions and garlic until they are translucent. Add the zucchini and paprika, and cook until throughout. The bay leaves should be added to the pan, and sprinkle with seasoning salt and pepper. Let the pot simmer covered for 10 minutes.

3. Combine the crème fraiche, and crumbled feta. Place the paprika-flavored vegetables into a dish for baking, and put the mix on top. Preheat the oven at 250°F and bake the vegetables under the grill's middle rack for between eight and 10 minutes.

Seafood-based dishes

1. Fish braised Shanghai

For 4 persons

Difficulty: Easy

Time to work: approximately. 40 minutes

Total production time Time of production: 50 minutes

Ingredients

The classic vegetable stock is 450 milliliters.

Bamboo shoots of 250 grams

150 grams of shiitake mushroom

125 g pork

100 ml soy sauce

40 ginger

8 tbsp of rapeseed oil

6 spring onions

5 cloves garlic

4 tbsp rice wine

2 Tbsp cornstarch

1 Sea bass

One very small onion

sugar

Preparation

1. Rinse the pork in water and then dry it. Cut it to thin strips.

2. Clean the shiitakes and take out the stems. Rinse the bamboo shoots and slice them into thin slices.

3. Peel off the garlic and chop it roughly. Peel the ginger and cut it into thin slices.

Peel off the onion, and cut it into small rings.

4. Rinse the fish then pat dry. Make multiple cuts on both sides , at an angle that extends to the bone.

5. Six tablespoons of oil are heated in the wok. In a wok, add two slices or more of ginger, and cook the fish for 3 to 4 minutes on both sides. The entire fish should be touching the oil. Get the fish out. Remove the ginger and oil.

6. Clean the wok then heat it up and add the rest of the oil. The meat should be cooked for a few minutes over high heat, then remove it.

7. Add the mushrooms and garlic to the and the remaining onions, and ginger into the wok. Stir fry for two minutes, with a stir.

8. Include the veggie stock and a teaspoon of sugar rice wine, as well as soy sauce into the wok. Place the fish and meat in the wok, and cook for 8 minutes covered on a medium-low flame.

9. Clean spring onions and cut them into two centimeter-long pieces. After eight minutes, flip the fish upside down and add the spring onions into the sauce. Cook for another 4 minutes.

10. Remove the fish from the water and set it on a platter. Mix some cornstarch and water and stir it into the sauce, and bring it to a simmer. Add salt and pepper, then drizzle over the fish.

2. Fish braised with tomatoes

For 2 persons

Difficulty: Easy

Time to work: approximately. 30 minutes

Total production time Time of production: 50 minutes

Ingredients

250 g fillet of fish (cod or monkfish)

Two cloves garlic finely chopped

2tomatoes

1onion finely chopped

1 green pepper

1 red pepper

One bunch of basil

1 leaf from a bay

1 tablespoon olive oil 1 tablespoon olive

1 Tbsp oregano

Salt and pepper

Preparation

1. The tomatoes are scalded for a couple of seconds, then rinse and peel them. Cut them into four pieces and then core. Clean them, then cut them into two pieces and then remove the seeds. Cut into strips.

2. Clean the fish and wipe dry. Cut into cubes of about 4x4 centimeters.

3. In the oil, heat it and sauté the garlic and onion. Add tomatoes, peppers bay leaves, oregano, bay leaves and let it simmer for two minutes. Add salt and pepper to taste. Place the fish over and cook, covered, for about 8 minutes.

4. Sprinkle with basil before serving. Potato wedges are great with it.

3. Fish that has been braised

For 4 persons

Difficulty: Easy

Time to work: approximately. 20 minutes

Time to produce 1 hour and 5 minutes

Ingredients

400 g of leek

White wine 125 ml dry

5 tall tomatoes

4 slices of fillets of fish

3 lemons

Three tablespoons of olive oil

Two cloves of garlic

Basil

rosemary

Dill

Salt and pepper

Preparation

1. Remove the fillets of fish. Sprinkle the juice from 1.5 lemons over the fish.

2. Clean the leek , then cut it into slices. Stir-fry the garlic and leek for around 10 minutes. Add salt and black pepper.

3. Distribute the vegetables into an oven-proof dish. Divide the tomatoes with the remainder of the lemons, and cut them to thin strips.

4. Salt the fish. Then together with lemons and tomatoes place them as scales over the leek. Add pepper, basil rosemary, salt and basil. Add the wine.

5. The oven should be heated to 180 degrees and cook the fish for 45 minutes.

6. Sprinkle the dill over the the top prior to serving and serve with baguette.

4. Red pepper fish

For 6 persons

Difficulty: Easy

Time to work: approximately. 20 minutes

Production time total Time of production: 1 hour

Ingredients

6 fillets of fish

2 red peppers

One glass of milk

A bit of mustard

Lemon juice

Salt and pepper

Abascos BT by BT

Preparation

1. Cut the peppers in half and cut them into strips. Grease a baking pan and put the peppers in it. Sprinkle citrus juice on the fillets of fish, and leave them to rest for 10 minutes. Salt and spice the fish fillets, then put them on top of the vegetables.

2. Make a sauce using milk as well as paprika and pepper. Add some mustard as well as Tabasco according to your taste. Serve this sauce on the fish.

3. Preheat the oven at 200 degrees C. Cook the fish for 30 to 40 minutes. Rice, herbal baguette and boiled potatoes work well together.

5. Braised Snoek

For 4 persons

Difficulty: Normal

Time to work: approx. 10 minutes

Total production time 20 minutes

Ingredients

4 large potatoes

4fish fillets (mackerel fillets)

4 onions

1 chili pepper

White bread

butter

Cayenne pepper

Salt and pepper

Preparation

1. Cook the fillets of fish with plenty of water. After that, you can break them into small pieces.

2. Peel and chop the onions roughly. Remove the seeds of the chili pepper, then

chop them finely. Peel, wash and chop the potatoes.

3. The butter should be melted in a saucepan. Add the onions and chili and cook. Then add the potatoes, and fry them as fries. Last, add the fish flakes and fry them well.

4. Add cayenne salt, pepper and cayenne. Serve with white bread.

6. Fish that has been braised in wine

For 8 people

Difficulty: Easy

The working time is approximately. 20 minutes

Time of production 1 hour and 5 minutes

Ingredients

1 kg fillet of salmon Peeled and weighed 1 kg of fish fillet

300 ml white wine dry

100 ml olive oil

50 grams white breadcrumbs

Four stalks of celery roughly chopped

4 spring onions cut into pieces

4 tomatoes, sliced

4 tbsp chopped parsley, chopped

3 toes garlic, crushed

2 large onions, cut into rings

2 lemons, cut

2 tablespoons lemon juice

2 tablespoons of dried oregano

Parsley chopped, to be used as garnish

Salt and pepper

Preparation

1. The oven should be heated to 180 degrees C. Then heat the olive oil to 2 tablespoons in a fry pan. In it, cook the onions for 3 minutes. Add spring onions garlic, parsley, garlic tomatoes and celery. Stir well and simmer for another five minutes.

2. Prepare a ovenproof flat dish along with the remaining oil. Place the fish fillets into the dish. Add oregano to the fish, and add the salt as well as pepper. The onion mixture is spread over the fish using a spoon . Place slices of lemon on the top.

3. Pour the juice of a lemon and the wine over it. Sprinkle breadcrumbs over the the top. Bake covered for approximately 45 minutes until the fish turns golden brown. Garnish with chopped chopped parsley, and serve.

7. Calamari cooked with tomatoes

For 4 persons

Difficulty: Easy

Time to work: approximately. 30 minutes

Production time total: 2hrs and 15 minutes

Ingredients

600 g squid. Cleanse

200 Ml dry white wine

4ripe tomatoes

3 shallots

3 tablespoons lemon juice

2 Tablespoons Olive Oil

2 tablespoons fresh chopped parsley

1 . A clove

1 2 tbsp finely chopped fresh basil

1 teaspoon of sugar

Salt and pepper

Preparation

1. Clean squids, then pat dry. The tubes can be cut into strips and then drizzle lemon juice over the top. Let them remain in the refrigerator for about an hour.

2. Wash tomatoes in cold water. Peel off the skin then cut into four pieces core and chop the pulp. Peel and chop the shallots and garlic.

3. In an oven. Steam the shallots until they become translucent. Incorporate the garlic, basil tomatoes, sugar, and basil and make a deglaze using white wine. Mix the squids in along with marinade. Cover and cook on low temperature up to 35- 40

mins. Add salt and pepper. then sprinkle with parsley, and serve. Baguette can be served with it.

8. Ravioli and salmon on white wine braised

For 4 persons

Difficulty: Normal

Time to work: approx. 45 minutes

Time to produce Time of production: 1 hour and 15 minutes

Ingredients

For the vegetable

250 ml vegetable stock

150 g of cream

Three tablespoons of olive oil

2 teaspoons mustard, medium hot

1 white cabbage

1 onion

1 teaspoon of flour

1 teaspoon of sugar

A bit of nuts

Salt and pepper

For the fish

600 g salmon fillet, skinless

2 tbsp butter lard

Some lemon peel

Additionally

400 g ravioli , with spinach filling

Five stalks of parsley leaf

Preparation

1. Cleanse the cabbage in the white and chop the stem into small strips. Peel and

chop the onion. In the meantime, heat the olive oil in a pan. In the same saucepan, fry the onion cubes as well as white cabbage strips in it. Sprinkle flour on this and let it sweat. Deglaze the dish with the vegetable stock and the cream. Add the mustard and stir and bring it to a boiling point and simmer covered for 10-12 minutes.

2. Wash the fillets of salmon thoroughly and dry them. Cut the fillets in narrow strips. The clarified butter is heated in a large pot. Fry the salmon with both sides of the fish for around two minutes. Sprinkle with salt, pepper as well as lemon juice.

3. Cook ravioli in salted water following the directions on the package. Let it run off. Rinse your parsley and shake dry , and cut the parsley leaves.

4. The cabbage should be seasoned by grating freshly grated nuts salt, pepper

and sugar and season with salt and sugar to your liking. Place the cabbage on the plates , then place the ravioli, as well as salmon pieces on top. Sprinkle the parsley on top.

9. Cod cooked in braised kale with mustard sauce

For 4 persons

Difficulty: Easy

Time to work: approximately. 30 minutes

Time to produce 1 hour 15 minutes

Ingredients

For the vegetable

600 g of green cabbage

200 ml vegetable stock

50 g bacon, perfectly diced

1 meter large onion

Salt and pepper

Maybe bread flour

For the fish

600 G Cod fillets

Four stems of Thyme

2 tablespoons vegetable oil

A little bit of flour

Salt and pepper

To make the sauce

200 ml vegetable stock

100ml of cream

100ml wine

50 grams of butter

25 grams of flour

4 EL Dijon mustard

Preparation

1. Peel the onions, then cut them in small pieces. Cut off the midrib of the leaves of the kale. Rinse, dry and then chop it roughly. The lard is heated in the pan. Fry the pork belly in dices as well as the kale and onions. Add salt and pepper and remove the kale with 200 ml vegetable stock. The kale should cook on moderate temperature for 35-45 minutes. If needed, tie it with breadcrumbs.

2. Make braids, then incorporate the flour. Allow it to simmer while you stir. Add gradually Riesling as well as cream, while stirring. Allow the mixture to simmer for at least 5 minutes. After that, mix into the Dijon mustard and then take it off the flame.

3. Wash the cod filletsthoroughly, dry them and add spice and salt. The fish fillets are seasoned with flour and heat 2 tablespoons oil on a pot and cook the fish for about four to five minutes each side.

4. Take the thyme out of the stems and put them in the pan. Serving the cod, kale and the thyme. Then serve the mustard sauce on top of it.

5. Serve with potatoes that have been cooked.

10. Conger eel that is braised in colorful vegetables

For 2 persons

Difficulty: Normal

Time to work: approximately. 45 minutes

Time to produce 1 hour and 10 minutes

Ingredients

125 ml fish stock

60 g zucchini, cut into balls

50ml white wine Dry

30 g of celery, cut into slices

30 grams Leek in rings

30 g parsley slices, root

10 black olives

four slices of fish conger eel

Two tablespoons tomatoes chopped

2 Tablespoons Olive Oil

2 cl Vermouth, Noilly Prat

1 carrot

1 shallot

1 . cloves of garlic cut into fine pieces

1/2 red pepper Cut into strips

Salt, curry, and pepper

Preparation

1. Take off the skin of the eel with an eel knife. The garlic and shallot are cooked into olive oil. Cut the vegetables and cook except for bell peppers, olives and tomato cubes, along with the eel slices for 3 minutes. Make a sauce by adding fish stock, Noilly Prat and white wine and then simmer in a covered pot for 15 minutes.

2. After 10 minutes After ten minutes, mix in the herb mixture along with olives and pepper strips. Add the tomato cubes right before serving, and fold them in gently. Add salt, pepper and curry.

3. Place all the veggies on a platter and put the fish pieces on the top. Saffron rice is a great choice with it.

11.Maltese style braised Squid

For 4 persons

Difficulty: Normal

Time to work: approx. 30 minutes

Total production time 2 hours

Ingredients

800 grams of Squid

500 ml tomatoes, happened

50 grams black olives, chopped or halved

White wine 25 ml

5 fillets of anchovy

4 toes garlic

4 m. Tomatoes, diced

3 teaspoons capers

1 large onion

A handful of parsley leaves chopped

olive oil

Lemon zest

Salt and pepper

Preparation

1. Prepare the pulpo: take off the beak. Cut the tentacles and body into bite-sized pieces, or keep them as is.

2. Cut the garlic and onion into cubes, then sauté in oil olive. Add the pulpo, and fry. The squid's fluid is lost in the process. Continue cooking and stirring until a pleasant aroma of roast is achieved as well as the liquid is evaporated. Add the white wine to the deglaze and then add the passata and tomatoes. Reduce the temperature and add capers, lemon zest, and olives If needed. Cook for about an

hour while keeping the lid closed. Add salt and pepper. When you are done add the parsley chopped.

3. It is great with white bread and pasta.

12. Salmon trout served with braised Chicory, curry and garam masala

For 4 persons

Difficulty: Normal

Time to work: approx. 10 minutes

Total production time Time of production: 30 minutes

Ingredients

50ml orange juice

4 fillets of salmon trout

4 perennial chicory

2 tablespoons oil

2 Tbsp butter

One packet lemon butter sauce

1 TEASPOON Curry

Salt and pepper

Preparation

1. Clean the chicory, then cut it into two halves. In an oven large enough to fry the chicory on one side. Sprinkle with salt and pepper and then deglaze by adding orange juice. Cover the pan, and allow it to simmer on simmering on a low heat for approximately 15 minutes.

2. The fish filets should be salt and peppered. Warm the oil in the frying pan, and cook the fillets on medium heat,

starting in the area of skin, and shorter before reaching the cooking point for the meat portion.

3. Prepare the sauce as per the directions on the package and add 1 spoon of the curry.

4. Pearl barley, risotto as well as celery work well together.

13. Octopus braised

For 3 persons.

Difficulty: Normal

Time to work: approximately. 30 minutes

Total production time 2 hours 20 minutes

Ingredients

1 kg octopus

250ml white wine, dry

4 Garlic cloves peeled and press

3Tomatoes, diced

3 bay leaves

2 sprigs of Thyme

2 onions 2 onions, finely chopped

1 . A bunch of parsley finely chopped

1 red pepper, diced

1 . A bunch of parsley finely chopped

1/2 teaspoon of cumin, finely crushed

olive oil

Chili pieces

Flour for dusting

Salt and pepper

Preparation

1. Remove the head from the octopus, below the eyes. The beak is pushed out of

its tentacle-like body. Cut off the head, above the eyes. Then turn it inside out , and wash it. Remove the skin that surrounds it. Clean everything.

2. Cook a casserole over medium-high heat, then place the octopus into it. In its own juice, simmer in a pot that is sealed for about 15 minutes. The octopus changes to a light reddish. Get the octopus out and separate tentacles. Cut each into three pieces. Reduce or split the head. Dust the flour on the pieces of octopus.

3. Take the liquid from the casserole. In the oven, heat oil. Add all ingredients, excluding Octopus, chili wine, pepper and salt and cook for five minutes. Add the octopus and add the wine, and stir again. Saute at a low setting for 1 to one and a half hours. After about an hour, you can test whether the octopus is soft. After that, season it to taste with chili pepper, salt and flakes of chili.

4. Baguette papas arrugadas, baguette, and roast potatoes are great with it.

14. Blue river hammer braised with Thai basil

For 4 persons

Difficulty: Difficult

The working time is approximately. 1 hour

Production time total Time of production: 3 hours

Ingredients

20 basil leaves

Six stems of fresh green pepper

4 large lobsters

4 Garlic cloves peeled and finely chopped

4 tbsp chicken stock

three small chilli peppers red crushed

3 tablespoons of oil from a vegetable

2 Bund basil

2 tbsp galangal, peeled, fine strips

Two tablespoons Thai rice whiskey

2 tbsp soy sauce, light

2 tbsp fish sauce

2 tbsp oyster sauce

pepper

To marinate the meat.

2 . 2 cloves garlic

Two small peppers red crushed

2 tbsp soy sauce, light

1 Tablespoon oyster sauce

1 tbsp ginger, peeled, fine strips

One tablespoon Thai rice whiskey

pepper

Preparation

1. To marinate Mix all the ingredients in the bowl. Split the river lobster lengthways, then devein. Clean using a clean kitchen towel. Put the lobsters in a bowl and pour your marinade on the lobsters. Allow to sit at room temperature for 2 hours.

2. In an oven-proof pan. Cook the garlic chopped in it at a low temperature. Then, remove the pot from flame and set the lobsters on top of each other and with their peels facing up. Include the basil stem, oyster sauce galangal and chicken stock, as well as soy sauce. Shake the pan so that the ingredients are evenly distributed. Cover the pan and cook on low heat for about three up to 4 minutes. Take off the lid and allow the steam to

escape briefly. The rice whiskey is heated and then flambe the lobsters using it. Then add the pan with pepper. Place the lid back on and cook for 20-30 minutes.

3. Get the lobster out and put it in a warm area. Reduce the sauce and then season by adding fish sauce. Remove the pan from the heat and then remove the basil.

4. Sprinkle salt on the sauce, then serve on the tails of lobster. Serve with crispy Thai the basil leaves.

15. Braised fish flyt with sour bamboo

For 2 persons

Difficulty: Normal

Working time: approximately. 30 minutes

Total production time: 30 mins

Ingredients

500 g of fish fillets

200g bamboo slices cut into slices and then pickled

8 tablespoons soy sauce, light

6 shallots

4Chili pods, red dry, pitted chopped

4 basil leaves

4 tablespoons oil

4 tbsp fish sauce

2 . 2 cloves garlic

2 stems lemongrass

2 teaspoons of salt

One bunch of spring onions

Preparation

1. Rinse, drain and chop the bamboo into strips.

2. Cut the garlic finely as well as chop the Thai shallots to make the paste. Get rid of the hard leaves from the lemongrass. Then, cut the white portion to rings. Then chop finely.

3. The garlic should be crushed with salt and a pinch in a mortar. Next, crush the chilies, shallots as well as the finely chopped piece of the lemongrass into the mortar.

4. Cut the remainder of the lemongrass. Then, smash it into a soft ball using the pest.

5. Cut the fillets of fish into pieces that are about 3 centimeters in length.

6. The peanut oil is heated inside the wok. The seasoning paste is cooked in it for approximately two minutes. Cook the

lemongrass leaves briefly. Put the salmon in the skillet, sprinkle with soy and fish sauce and fry for 2 to three minutes or until the fish becomes white and becomes browned. Mix in the bamboo.

7. Pour hot water on the fish and mix. The fish should only be covered in half. Let it sit for approximately 3 minutes on a low temperature, rotating at least once during the process.

8. Mix in lemon basil, along with spring onions. Sprinkle chili rings on top and serve. It is delicious with rice that is fragrant.

16. Squid tubes braised with barley and the filling of chard

For 2 persons

Difficulty: Normal

Working time: approximately. 30 minutes

Time to produce 1 hour and 5 minutes

Ingredients

200 ml of broth, strong

40 grams of pearl barley

3 Squid

Two cloves of garlic

two leaves of chard with no stems

One can of tomato

Lemon juice

Salt and pepper

Preparation

1. The pearl barley is cooked slowly and then added to the broth.

2. Rinse the tubes using cold water, and then remove the backbone if required. Cut the tubing into cubes. Wash the leaves thoroughly and dry. Cut into fine cubes. Peel the garlic, and then slice into pieces.

3. Allow the pearl barley to cook and cool, then mix it together with garlic Swiss the chard as well as squid cubes. Salt and pepper it and add them to the tubes. Cover with kitchen twine or toothpicks.

4. The tomatoes are heated and placed on the tubes on the top. Salt, pepper and drizzle the lemon juice. Cover and simmer the tomato sauce on the stove at a simmer for approximately 45 minutes. Change the pot at intervals.

5. Remove the wooden sticks and twine from the cooking tubs. Slice the tomato sauce into slices or cut into half on an angle. Sprinkle the tomato sauce with salt and pepper before serving.

17. Octopus braised

For 4 persons

Difficulty: Normal

Working time: approximately. 25 minutes

Time to produce 1 hour and 25 minutes

Ingredients

500 g of squid

50 grams red peppers

16 olives, black, pitted

Three tablespoons of olive oil

1 pepper

1 . A clove

1 tbsp, tomato paste

1 teaspoon of oregano

Half a bunch of fresh parsley

Salt and pepper

Preparation

1. Cut the octopus into 1-centimeter pieces and cut into slices. The parsley can be cut into smaller pieces. Slice the pepper red as well as clove of garlic into smaller pieces. Find the chili pepper and cut it into smaller pieces.

2. The olive oil is heated in a skillet. Cook the chili pepper as well as the garlic and bell pepper in a medium heat for a couple of minutes. Add the octopus , olives, parsley oregano, salt tomato paste, and 50ml of water. Mix thoroughly. Cover and simmer. Stir occasionally and add water as needed. The octopuses can take anywhere between 1 and 2 hours.

3. It is delicious with hard-boiled or white bread. polenta.

Soups / stews / side dishes

1. Soup for carrots and scamorza

For 12 people

Difficulty: Normal

Time to work: approximately. 45 minutes

Time to produce 1 hour 30 minutes

Ingredients

1.25 kg of carrots (thick)

400 G shallots

250 g smoked scamorza

The basil leaf is large and it's 6 inches long.

3 stems of oregano

3 tablespoons lemon juice

Two dried chilies from red.

2 1 tbsp rosemary needles

2 Tablespoons Olive Oil

1 Liter of juice from carrots

1 liter vegetable stock

1 red pepper

1 teaspoon of orange peel (finely grated)

sea-salt

Preparation

1. Remove the dirt from the carrots. Cut the shallots as well as carrots into three cm pieces. Place them in the juice pan of the oven. Add 500 ml of the juice of a carrot rosemary, oregano, rosemary and chili peppers. Season with salt. Preheat the oven until 250 ° and then simmer at the lowest setting for 40-45 minutes or

until the liquid is nearly evaporated. The oven's door should be opened each now and then.

2. Remove the pepper from its dirt, chop extremely finely, and mix in orange peel and olive oil. Slice the cheese off the rind, then thinly slice and mix in the oil from the orange.

3. Once the carrot mixture has been cooled, blend thoroughly. Pour in the vegetable broth as well as the rest of the juice of the carrot and cook for around 10 minutes. Add lemon juice and salt as needed. Just before serving chop the basil into thin strips. Mix the basil with the scamorza. Put the cheese first on the soup dish, then pour the soup into it.

2. Stew made with lamb and chestnuts

For 4 persons

Difficulty: Normal

Working time: approximately. 20 minutes

Total production time The total production time is 50 minutes

Ingredients

1 kilogram of lamb's leg

500 ml of meat stock

700 grams of pork sausage

500 g of chestnuts

500 g potatoes

250 grams of carrots

2 Tablespoons Olive Oil

1 pepper 1 pepper, red

1/2 lemon 1/2 lemon, juice and zest

Salt and pepper

Preparation

1. Chop the chestnuts into pieces and cook them on the stove at 200°C for approximately 30 minutes. Then, take them off.

2. Cut the lamb into cubes. Peel the carrots, potatoes and onions, then cut into cubes. Wash the cabbage savoy before you cut it into pieces. Cut off the zest of the lemon, and then squeeze the juice.

3. Steam the onion and pepper pods in oil until they are translucent. Then, slowly adding the chestnuts, potatoes meat, carrots, lemon zest and savoy cabbage. Add broth to it and bring it to the simmer. Cover the pot and allow to simmer for around an hour. Add salt, pepper, and juice of a lemon.

3. Vanilla carrots

For 3 people.

Difficulty: Easy

Time to work: approximately. 15 minutes

Total production time Time of production: 30 minutes

Ingredients

70 ml vegetable stock

One bunch of green carrots and one with a couple of red

1 vanilla pod

1 teaspoon butter

1/2 teaspoon of cane sugar

Some lemon peel

Preparation

1. Take the greens out of the carrots. Leave the green. Peel and cut the carrots in half.

2. Caramelize the butter and sugar in a large saucepan and then add the carrots. Cut the vanilla pod into pieces and scrape the pulp out and then add it to the carrots along with lemon zest. Add vegetable stock to the deglazing process when the carrots are coated all sides. Then cover and simmer for around 15 minutes.

4. Thuringian napkin dumplings

For 4 persons

Difficulty: Normal

Working time: approximately. 30 minutes Total

Production time: 1 hour 30 minutes

Ingredients

500 ml milk

275 grams of bread toasted, with no crust

110 g semolina

100g butter soft

50 g chives and 50 g parsley Very finely chopped

4 m.-sized eggs

3m shallots

Allspice d'Espelette

nutmeg

Salt and pepper

Preparation

1. Slice toast bread into very small pieces. Sauté the shallots with butter until translucent . Allow to cool.

2. The milk and semolina are brought to a boil, then allow to stand for ten minutes. Incorporate the softened butter, and,

piece by piece, the egg whites that have been beat. Add pieces of bread, the herbs and shallots. Sprinkle with pimento d'Espelette, nutmeg salt and pepper.

3. Divide the dumplings and place it on napkins.

4. Allow it to cook in the steamer 35-40 minutes at 95 ° and in the water for 30 minutes. Unwrap it, cool briefly, then stir it in butter.

5. Pureed parsley root

For 4 persons

Difficulty: Normal

Time to work: approx. 10 minutes

Total time to produce: 20 minutes

Ingredients

100 ml poultry stock

100ml of cream

Four large roots of parsley

1 onion

A little butter

Preparation

1. Peel and chop roughly the parsley roots. Peel the onions and then finely chop them.

2. In a short time, sweat the onion cubes as well as the parsley root in butter. Incorporate the fresh thyme. After approximately three minutes, remove the thyme and deglaze it by adding the chicken stock. Allow the roots to cook over the lowest temperature.

3. Pour in the cream after the vegetables have been cooked. After that, blend it finely with a hand blender.

6. Baked herb potatoes

For 1 per

Difficulty: Easy

The working time is approximately. 15 minutes

Time of production Time of production: 1 hour

Ingredients

10 g of butter

2 potatoes

Herbs, mixed

Mixed spices

Salt and pepper

Preparation

1. Clean the potatoes, slice them in half lengthwise, then place them without peeling on baking sheets. The cut areas

should be sprinkled with as many herbs as you can.

2. Salt and pepper, and then put the butter flake onto each of the potatoes.

3. The oven bakes for approximately 45 minutes at 220 degrees.

7. Confit onions

For 6 persons

Difficulty: Easy

Time to work: approximately. 10 minutes

Total production time: 40 mins

Ingredients

200 ml olive oil

20 pearl onions

4 sprigs of Thyme

2 bay leaves

2 rosemary sprigs

2 tablespoons sugar brown

1/2 toe garlic

Salt and pepper

Preparation

1. Cut off a little bit of the roots and tips of the onions , then peel the onions. Make a oven-safe dish in which the onions can sit.

2. In the bay leaves, put them in it first, then add the garlic and herbs sprigs and finally the onions. Sprinkle salt, pepper and sugar on top, then pour into the oil until the onions are only barely covered.

3. The oven should be heated to 80°C, then prepare the onion at 160 degrees C for around 30 minutes. The onions shouldn't provide any resistance when you pierce them.

8. Honey onions

For 6 persons

Difficulty: Normal

Working time: approximately. 30 minutes

Time to produce Time of production: 1 hour and 30 minutes

Ingredients

1 kg onions small and round

250 ml of water in warm

40 ginger root

Ten tablespoons of olive oil

Four stalks of celery small

4 bay leaves

2 tbsp honey

Two teaspoons salt

One can of saffron

1 cinnamon stick

1 teaspoon black pepper, black

Preparation

1. Remove the onion. Chop the celery into small slices. Peel and then grate the ginger. Mix all the ingredients apart from the honey and water, within a large casserole. In warm water, dissolve honey before you add to.

2. The oven should be preheated to 175°F. Cook the pot that is closed within the oven approximately. sixty to ninety minutes, on the lowest shelf. Rotate the rack once or twice, then let it cool.

9. Mashed carrots and potatoes

For 2 persons

Difficulty: Easy

Time to work: approximately. 20 minutes

Total production time: 40 mins

Ingredients

240 g potatoes

100g carrots, peeled

30g parsnips peeled, 30g

30 milliliters sweet cream

1 leaf of a bay

1 tbsp basil pesto

1 tbsp almondscut into slices and then roasted

Chili salt

nutmeg

White, pepper, ground

Preparation

1. Peel the potatoes and place them in salted water along with the carrots and parsnips. Add the bay leaf , and cook until tender.

2. The almonds are roasted on a low flame, without fat or oil. Warm the whipped cream.

3. Take the vegetables out of the water, and then take off the bay leaves. The lid should be allowed to steam with the lid on halfway. Make a mash by making the hot cream using the potato mashing. Sprinkle with chili salt, nutmeg , and pepper, and then fold into the pesto made of basil.

4. Sprinkle with the almond flake before serving.

10. A stew of meat and potatoes with carrots

For 6 persons

Difficulty: Normal

Time to work: approximately. 30 minutes

Total production time 2 hours

Ingredients

600 g of beef

600 g potatoes

400ml of water

60 grams of butter

2 . 2 cloves garlic

2 tbsp tomato paste

1 onion

1 carrot

1 tbsp vegetable fat

Spices can be added at the discretion of the user.

Salt and pepper

Preparation

1. Cut the potatoes into small pieces and meat. Chop onion and carrot into smaller pieces. Peel the garlic.

2. In a large skillet cook the oil on moderate temperature. In it, cook the beef for about five to seven minutes, until it's brown all over. Spice it up with pepper, spices and salt.

3. Place the meat in the potatoes. Place the onion and garlic over the top.

4. Mix tomato paste with warm water in the bowl. Pour it into the saucepan, so that it's half full. Add butter to the saucepan.

5. Cover and bake on the stove at 180 degrees C for 90 minutes.

6. Let the stew sit within the oven 10-15 minutes. Serve it with salad.

11. Gyro soup

For 4 persons

Difficulty: Easy

Time to work: approximately. 30 minutes

Total production time: 50 mins

Ingredients

500 g of peppers

400 g pork slices

400ml beef stock

400 G canned tomatoes

200ml of cream

100 g creme fraiche

6 tbsp olive oil

6 cl Metaxa

4 - 5 tbsp gyros spice

2 tbsp tomato paste

2 tbsp balsamic vinegar

2 Tbsp chopped chopped parsley

2 tbsp chopped fresh basil

1 large vegetable onion

1 red hot pepper

One tablespoon sugar

1 teaspoon oregano

1 teaspoon sweet pepper 1 teaspoon sweet

A pinch of salt and pepper

Preparation

1. Sprinkle the pork strips with the bowl with three teaspoons olive oil, and 2 to 3 tablespoons of the gyros spice. The meat should be marinated for at least 30 mins.

2. Clean and cut the bell peppers. Cut into pieces. Peel the onions, then cut them into tiny cubes that are coarse. Slice the bell peppers in smaller pieces.

3. Finely chop the basil and parsley.

4. In the pan, heat it up and cook the gyros on all sides.

5. Take the cooked meat out of the pan and add 2 to 3 spoons of olive oil. The onion and pepper pieces within the hot oil. Include the tomato puree. In the end, deglaze everything with metaxa and beef stock.

6. Include two teaspoons balsamic vinegar two teaspoons of Gyros spice tomato cans, pepper sugar, oregano salt and pepper.

7. Then add the meat, to the pot and simmer on moderate heat for about 30 minutes. Then you should add the crème fraiche and cream. Continue cooking the soup for 10 minutes, stirring it and serving.

12. Lentil soup served alongside sausages

For 2 persons

Difficulty: Easy

Time to work: approximately. 10 minutes

Total time to produce: 40 minutes

Ingredients

300 G brown lentils

80 g bacon cubes

4 medium-sized potatoes

3 sausages

3 tablespoons 3 tbsp. rapeseed oil

2 carrots

1 liter vegetable stock

1 onion

1 leaf from a bay

1 tablespoon balsamic vinegar

1 teaspoon of majoran white pepper

1/2 stick of leek

1/4 cup celery

A pinch of salt

Preparation

1. Peel and chop carrots, celery, potatoes and onions. Cleanse the leek, then cut it into small pieces. Slice the sausages.

2. Prepare some oil in an enormous saucepan. Quickly fry the bacon cubes within the fat. The cut ingredients are cooked in pieces. Incorporate the balsamic vinegar and mustard. Then, deglaze the soup with vegetable stock. Add the bay leaf, lentils, spices, and a pinch sugar into the soup, and mix well.

3. Soup of lentils is prepared on medium heat for about 35 or 40 mins. Sprinkle chopped parsley on top of the soup, and serve.

13. Pointed cabbage tomato stew containing minced meat

For 4 persons

Difficulty: Easy

Time to work: approximately. 10 minutes

Total production time 35 minutes

Ingredients

600 g of pointed cabbage

500 grams minced meat

400 G canned tomatoes

200 g Herbal Creme Fraiche

150 mg beef boillon

3 tablespoons of 3 tbsp. rapeseed oil

Two cloves of garlic

1 onion

1 leaf of a bay

1/2 teaspoon cumin, marjoram, sea salt, nutmeg, sweet paprika, pepper

Preparation

1. Slice the garlic cloves as well as onions. Cut the pointed cabbage in quarters cut off the stalk, then chop into smaller pieces.